The Wild World of Animals

Deer

Graceful Grazers

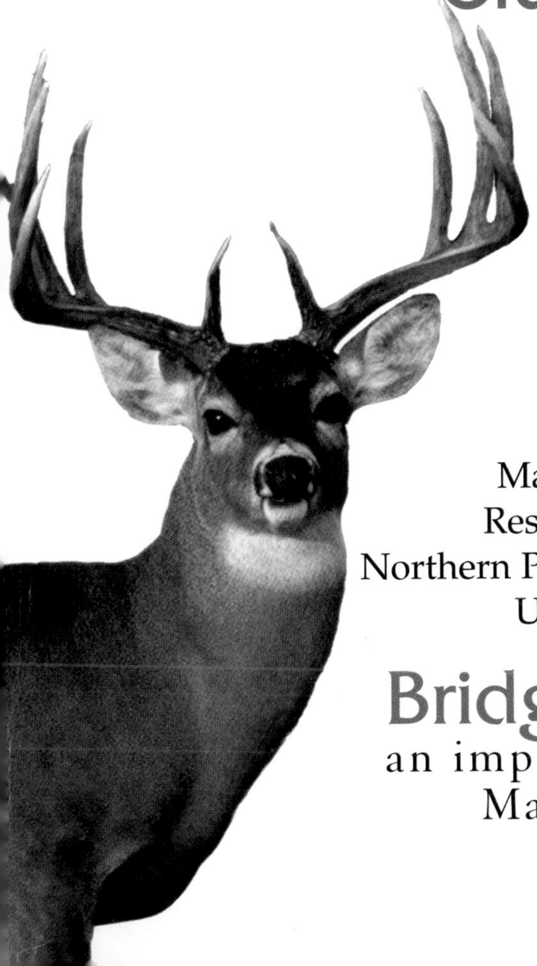

by Jody Sullivan

Consultant:
Marsha A. Sovada, Ph.D.
Research Wildlife Biologist
Northern Prairie Wildlife Research Center
U.S. Geological Survey

Bridgestone Books
an imprint of Capstone Press
Mankato, Minnesota

Bridgestone Books are published by Capstone Press
151 Good Counsel Drive, P.O. Box 669, Mankato, Minnesota 56002
http://www.capstone-press.com

Library of Congress Cataloging-in-Publication Data
Sullivan, Jody.
   Deer : graceful grazers / by Jody Sullivan.
   p. cm.—(The wild world of animals)
   Summary: A brief introduction to deer, describing their physical characteristics,
   habitats, young, food, predators, and relationship to people.
   Includes bibliographical references (p. 24) and index.
   ISBN 0-7368-1394-2 (hardcover)
   1. Deer—Juvenile literature. [1. Deer.] I. Title. II. Series.
QL737.U55 S85 2003
599.65—dc21   2001008150

Editorial Credits
Megan Schoeneberger, editor; Karen Risch, product planning editor; Linda Clavel,
   designer; Kelly Garvin, photo researcher

Photo Credits
Ann & Rob Simpson, 4
Corbis (texture), cover, 2, 3, 6, 10, 14, 18, 20, 22, 23, 24
Corbis/Dave G. Houser, 20
Erwin and Peggy Bauer/Bruce Coleman Inc., cover
James P. Rowan, 10
Jay Ireland & Georgienne E. Bradley, 6
Jim Rogers, 8
Kent & Donna Dannen, 12
Marv Binegar Photography, 14
Norvia Behling, 16
PhotoDisc, Inc., 1
Tom & Pat Leeson, 18

Table of Contents

antlers

fallow deer

hoof

ankle

4

Deer

Deer have big eyes and ears. They have long necks and long legs. All deer have four toes on each leg. The two middle toes form hooves. The other two toes are on the ankle. Most male deer have antlers. Male deer usually are larger than female deer.

ankle
the place where the leg connects to the foot

moose

FUN FACTS

The moose is the largest member of the deer family. Moose can be more than 8 feet (2.4 meters) tall.

6

Deer Are Mammals

Deer are mammals. Mammals are warm-blooded and have a backbone. Female mammals give birth to live young. Young mammals drink milk from their mothers. Mammals usually have hair or fur. Most deer have brown or gray hair.

warm-blooded
having a body temperature that stays the same

elk

A Deer's Habitat

Deer live in Asia, Europe, North America, and South America. Many deer live near forests. Other deer are found on mountains or in deserts. Some deer live in or near cities. Most large deer are found in cold habitats. Most small deer stay in warm habitats.

habitat
the place where an animal lives

Most female deer do not have antlers. But both male and female reindeer have antlers.

10

3 1833 04434 9808

mule deer

Antlers

Antlers grow on most male deer after spring. Antlers are made of bone. They grow quickly. Fuzz called velvet covers new antlers. Velvet is made of tiny hairs. It falls off after a few months. The antlers last about nine months before they fall off too.

mule deer

What Do Deer Eat?

Deer are herbivores. They eat mostly plants such as grass, leaves, and flowers. They also eat small branches. A deer has front teeth on only its bottom jaw. It uses these teeth to cut grass and stems. A deer's back teeth grind food.

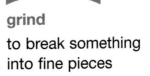

grind
to break something
into fine pieces

elk

FUN FACTS

Most male deer are called bucks. Most female deer are called does. Their young are called fawns. But moose, elk, and reindeer have different names. Males are bulls, females are cows, and their young are calves.

Mating and Birth

Male and female deer mate during fall. Males fight each other to mate with a female. They lock antlers together until one of the males gets tired. The winner then mates with the female. Females give birth to young in spring. A female usually has one or two young at a time.

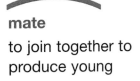

mate
to join together to produce young

white-tailed deer fawn

Fawns

Most young deer are called fawns. Most fawns have white spots on their brown hair. Their eyes are open at birth. Fawns can stand and walk shortly after birth. Fawns hide until they can keep up with their mother. Fawns must be able to run from predators.

predator
an animal that hunts
and eats other animals

white-tailed deer

18

FUN FACTS

White-tailed deer lift their tail when they sense danger. The bright white hair on the underside of the tail warns other deer.

Running from Danger

Deer have many predators. Wolves, coyotes, and cougars hunt deer in North America. Wolves and tigers hunt deer in Asia. Deer use their sense of smell and good hearing to avoid predators. Deer stand very still when they hear danger. They then run quickly to safety.

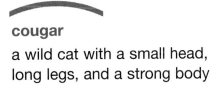

cougar

a wild cat with a small head, long legs, and a strong body

20

reindeer

Deer and People

People in North America hunt deer for meat and antlers. American Indians once made clothing out of deer skin. People in northern Europe and Asia get milk and meat from reindeer. They also use them to pull sleds. One reindeer can pull a 300-pound (136-kilogram) sled.

Hands On: Hear like a Deer

A deer's excellent hearing helps it hear predators. Its large ears gather sound. Try this activity to test your hearing.

What You Need

A TV or other source of soft noise
Two paper plates
Scissors

What You Do

1. Turn on the TV. Keep the sound quiet. Sit quietly and listen to the sounds around you. Think about how much you can hear.
2. Cut a small triangle out of the edge of each paper plate. The cut-out area should fit around your ear.
3. Hold one paper plate just behind each ear. Sit quietly and listen.

There should be a difference in the sounds you hear. The plates allow more sound to reach your ears. A deer's ears work in the same way.

Words to Know

antler (ANT-lur)—a bony growth on the head of male deer and some female deer; deer are the only animals that have antlers.

fawn (FAWN)—a young deer

habitat (HAB-uh-tat)—the place where an animal lives

herbivore (HUR-buh-vor)—an animal that eats mostly plants

jaw (JAW)—a part of the mouth used to grab, bite, and chew

mammal (MAM-uhl)—a warm-blooded animal that has a backbone and feeds milk to its young

mate (MATE)—to join together to produce young; deer mate during the fall.

predator (PRED-uh-tur)—an animal that hunts and eats other animals

Read More

Berendes, Mary. *Deer.* Nature Books. Chanhassen, Minn.: Child's World, 2000.

Frisch, Aaron. *Deer.* Northern Trek. Mankato, Minn.: Smart Apple Media, 2000.

Jaffe, Elizabeth D. *Deer Have Fawns.* Animals and Their Young. Minneapolis: Compass Point Books, 2002.

Internet Sites

Canadian Wildlife Service—Hinterland Who's Who— White-Tailed Deer
http://www.cws-scf.ec.gc.ca/hww-fap/deer/deer.html

The Deer Domain
http://www.deerdomain.com

Index